Contents

Introduction
Are you allergy-prone?   4

1 Allergies and the immune system
Causes and diagnosis   6

2 Allergic illnesses
Sneezes, wheezes and other discomforts   14

3 Allergens
Where they are found   26

4 Treating allergies
Soothing and preventative medicines   34

5 Living with allergies
Risk reduction and being prepared   46

Glossary   60

Resources   62

Index   63

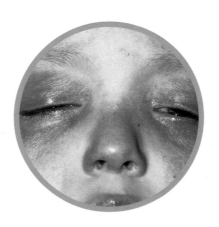

Introduction
Are you allergy-prone?

Your chances of developing an allergy depend on your genetic makeup and on your exposure to substances that can cause an allergy. The World Allergy Organization estimates that between 30 and 50 per cent of the global population are at risk of developing an allergy. Allergies cause a variety of illnesses that can affect your whole body. The most common allergic illnesses include hay fever (allergic rhinitis), asthma and sinusitis. The World Health Organization estimates that asthma affects nearly 150 million people, and allergic rhinitis affects more than 115 million people worldwide.

Allergies are uncomfortable and distressing, and can also be serious illnesses. Asthma is responsible for approximately 180,000 deaths per year worldwide. Another allergic condition called anaphylaxis is much rarer and can also be fatal; approximately 100 people die from anaphylaxis caused by food allergies each year in the USA. Allergies are also expensive. The World Allergy Organization estimates that approximately $20 billion are spent globally each year on allergic rhinitis alone. This includes the costs of medication, time off work and visiting a doctor.

Breathing, eating and ...
You may be allergic to something that you breathe in, like pollen, or something that you eat, like strawberries.

Allergies are sometimes said to be a disease of the modern Western world. Allergies are indeed a growing problem for industrialized countries. It seems that the higher your standard of living, the more likely you are to suffer from an allergy. This trend is illustrated by the rates of asthma (a common allergic illness) around the world. The highest incidence of asthma is found in Australia and New Zealand, whereas the lowest rates are found in poorer countries such as Albania, China, Eastern Europe and India.

There are many theories as to why there is such a large difference in the numbers of people affected by allergies around the world. People in industrialized nations now spend about 90 per cent of their time indoors. Indoor environments are not only comfortable for people, but ideal for certain allergens (allergy-causing substances) like moulds and dust mites. Another factor may be the poor air quality of industrialized areas. It may even be that our modern standards of cleanliness make us more vulnerable to developing allergies.

... Touching
Another way of coming into contact with an allergy-causing substance is by touch, as in the case of detergents.

Your risk of developing an allergic illness is affected by many factors. In this book, we start by looking at the mechanisms that cause allergies to occur, how your body responds if you have an allergy and how allergies are diagnosed. We then look at different types of allergic illnesses and their effects. Chapter 3 investigates the substances that cause allergies and where to find them. Chapter 4 looks at common treatments for allergies and Chapter 5 considers ways of minimizing the impact of allergies on your life and the different factors you need to be aware of when you are trying to reduce your exposure to allergy-causing substances.

1 Allergies and the immune system
Causes and diagnosis

Having an allergic illness can be very unpleasant. Although allergies rarely cause irreversible damage, they can be a source of constant irritation and discomfort. Allergies occur when your immune system (the system that protects your body from infection) mistakes a harmless substance for something dangerous. Under normal conditions your immune system is very good at telling the difference between harmless substances and things like viruses, bacteria and parasites that could cause you harm. But when you develop an allergy, your body reacts to harmless substances such as pollen or pet dander as if they were dangerous and produces the symptoms of allergy.

'I've got this nut allergy thing – you know – one peanut and it's curtains. Well nearly; I have to get to hospital pretty quickly. I have to be really careful what I eat.'
(Jordan)

Allergies can cause serious problems. They range in severity from allergies to insect stings and some foods, which can be fatal (these are very rare), to asthma, which can be mild or severe, and more minor conditions such as hay fever, which causes discomfort and aggravation during the pollen season.

Inheriting an allergic tendency

Your chances of developing an allergy depend on your genes and your environment. Some people inherit a tendency to develop allergic reactions through their genes. You may find that one member of a family has hay fever, another eczema and another asthma. Sometimes one individual may be unlucky enough to have more than one condition. This tendency to develop allergies is called

'I get hay fever in the spring. I sneeze, my eyes run. I hate it. I have to stay indoors as much as possible – boring.'
(Toni, telephone sales manager)

'atopy', and seems to be caused by slight differences in the gene responsible for the production of a particular antibody called IgE. Antibodies are protein molecules produced by your immune system, which are responsible for destroying bacteria, viruses and parasites.

Inheriting this alteration to the antibody IgE does not necessarily mean that you will develop an allergy. In order to develop an allergy you also have to be exposed to something in your environment that stimulates the allergy to occur. This may involve something as simple as coming into contact with a large amount of a substance that can cause an allergy (such substances are called allergens). It may also depend on other substances in the environment, such as chemicals or pollution, which make the antibody more likely to react to an allergen.

'My mother, uncle and two of my brothers have allergies. I only get a skin rash when I eat strawberries so it's fairly easy to avoid it, but one of my brothers has asthma, eczema and hay fever, so he suffers quite a lot.' (Jade, hairdresser)

Unwanted Inheritance

A tendency to develop allergies can be inherited. Sometimes several members of one family have allergic illnesses.

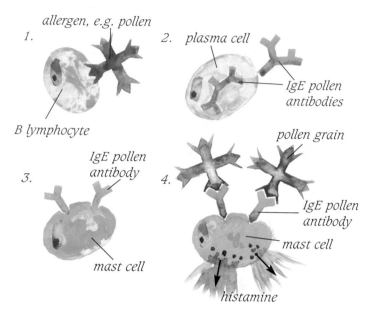

1. allergen, e.g. pollen

B lymphocyte

2. plasma cell

IgE pollen antibodies

3. IgE pollen antibody

mast cell

4. pollen grain

IgE pollen antibody

mast cell

histamine

Allergic response

1. A B-lymphocyte grabs hold of a pollen grain, which is mistaken for a virus or bacterium.

2. The B-lymphocyte goes to a lymph node and changes into a plasma cell, making large amounts of pollen IgE antibodies.

3. In the bloodstream, the pollen IgE antibodies attach themselves to mast cells. The body is now ready to react.

4. The next time the body comes into contact with the allergen, IgE anti-bodies attach themselves to mast cells, which produce the chemical histamine. Histamine causes the allergy symptoms.

Antibodies and allergy

For an allergy to develop, your immune system must become sensitive to the substance that causes the allergy (the allergen). Two things need to occur. Firstly, your body has to come into contact with an allergen. This can happen when you breathe in a certain substance, or eat something, or when something rubs against your skin or is injected into your body (if you are stung by a bee, for example). Secondly, your immune system must make a mistake and react to the harmless substance as if it were a dangerous bacterium, virus or parasite.

Lymphocytes (white blood cells) guard your body against infection. They travel around the body looking for bacteria, viruses and parasites that could cause you harm. When they find a substance that they do not recognize as being part of your body, they react quickly to destroy the invader. There are two types of lymphocyte, B-lymphocytes and T-lymphocytes. B-lymphocytes are involved in allergic reactions. When a B-lymphocyte finds an unknown particle, it makes a record of the substance and returns to a lymph node where it changes into a new type of cell called a plasma cell and releases large amounts of antibodies into your bloodstream.

There are several types of antibody but the antibody particularly associated with allergies is called Immuno-globulin E (IgE). When IgE is released into the bloodstream it attaches itself to special cells called mast cells. Your immune system is now sensitive to the substance caught by the B-lymphocytes and, if they have made a mistake and reacted to a normally harmless substance, you have now started to develop an allergy.

Allergic reactions

If you have an allergy, you may experience:

- runny or blocked nose (hay fever)
- itchy or watery eyes (hay fever)
- sneezing (hay fever)
- cough (asthma)
- shortness of breath (asthma)
- wheezing (asthma)
- tight feeling across the chest (asthma)
- diarrhoea
- vomiting
- drop in blood pressure.

It can take a week or more for the mast cells to become primed with IgE. However, once you have been sensitized in this way, your body will respond quickly the next time it detects the allergen. Your body will release large amounts of IgE into your system and your mast cells, now ready for action, will release large amounts of a chemical called histamine into your bloodstream in order to fight what is considered to be a dangerous invader. It is histamine that causes the symptoms of allergy. It makes your blood vessels expand and leak fluid, and it can also make your airways narrow; a rash (often called hives) may develop, and you may feel your heart beat faster.

How strongly you react to an allergen depends on how much histamine is released by your mast cells and which part of your body is affected. Some allergies caused by things such as bee stings can result in so much histamine being released into the bloodstream that the whole body is affected, and this can be fatal. This type of allergy is called anaphylaxis. Allergies to substances like pollen, house dust mites, pet hair and moulds are usually less severe and cause conditions such as asthma, hay fever, perennial rhinitis and eczema.

Diagnosing allergies

If you visit your doctor with a problem that could be caused by an allergy, he or she will listen to your description of what happens and ask questions such as: How long have you had the problem? Does anything make it better or worse? If the doctor suspects that you have an allergy-related illness, you will probably be prescribed an appropriate treatment or medicine. If this doesn't provide relief, or if your allergy is causing severe problems, you may be sent for tests to try to find out which allergen causes your symptoms. Identifying the cause of your allergy can help you to eliminate it from your environment and can help your doctor to prescribe the most effective treatment.

Skin tests

These sensitive tests involve contact between a tiny amount of allergen and your skin. If you have antibodies to the allergen, your skin will react by producing a raised, red, swollen area, which may be itchy. This is called a weal. The larger the weal, the more sensitive you are to the allergen. Skin tests are not appropriate for people suspected of having a severe allergic reaction (anaphylaxis), because any contact with an allergen can be life-threatening for individuals with these rare forms of allergy. There are four main types of skin test:

⊛ Skin prick test: A number of allergens are dropped onto your skin, at marked positions. The skin under the allergen droplets is then pricked lightly to bring it into closer contact with the allergen. Any reaction is usually visible in 20 minutes.

⊛ Intradermal skin test: More sensitive than skin prick testing, this is sometimes used if skin prick tests have not shown any reaction but allergy is still suspected. A small quantity of allergen is injected into the top

Skin prick testing

Skin prick tests are the most common form of skin tests. They can help doctors work out exactly which substances a patient is allergic to.

layers of the skin. It can feel a little like having a gnat bite. Any reaction is usually visible in 20 minutes.

- Skin scratch testing: Very similar to the skin prick test, this involves a small scratch being made in the upper layers of skin before the suspected allergen is applied. Any reaction is usually visible within 20 minutes.

- Skin patch tests: These are used to test allergens suspected of causing contact eczema. The allergen is placed on a pad, which is then left on the skin for approximately 2 days. The skin is then observed to see if any of the allergens have caused eczema to occur.

These tests can be very useful in identifying what you are allergic to. However, sometimes the results can be misleading as, for instance, a substance that produces a skin reaction may not necessarily produce allergic asthma or hay fever, and substances that cause asthma or hay fever may not produce a skin reaction. Similarly, substances that cause food allergies may not necessarily cause a skin reaction.

Allergic to cats

'I first started wheezing when I was 8 and I went to stay with my aunt who bred Persian cats. I loved being there: the cats were beautiful and I helped groom them every day. It wasn't the first time I had been there – I had helped before, and the doctor reckons that I must have been sensitized before the wheezing started. It started gradually and just got worse and worse. Mum took me home and the doctor sent me for skin prick tests. I reacted immediately to cat dander. I have to avoid cats and carry an inhaler with me in case I start wheezing.'
(Mya, aged 16)

Blood tests

Blood tests are sometimes used to confirm skin prick tests or, if the allergy is severe, instead of skin tests, because of the risk of anaphylaxis. Blood tests measure the amount of the antibody IgE in your bloodstream while your symptoms are at their worst. This can show that an illness is due to allergy rather than another cause.

Occasionally doctors ask for a blood reaction test, where a small piece of tissue paper coated with an allergen is added to a sample of your blood serum under a microscope. If the antibodies in your blood are sensitive to the allergen, they will rush to the allergen and start to react with it. Analysis of this reaction can give a good idea of how severe the allergy is and if the individual is at risk of anaphylaxis.

Challenge tests

These tests are only usually carried out if other tests have given conflicting evidence. They are much less common than skin and blood tests and are only performed in special centres or hospitals, because they carry a small risk of producing an anaphylactic reaction. The tests reproduce the allergic illness under controlled conditions, by bringing the person into contact with a suspected allergen and monitoring the outcome.

Blood testing
Blood tests can show if you have lots of the allergy antibody IgE in your blood.

- Bronchoprovocation test (bronchial challenge test): Your lung function is checked; then you breathe in a small amount of a substance that provokes an asthma attack and your lung function is checked again to see if your airways have narrowed.

- Nasal challenge test (for allergic rhinitis): You breathe in small amounts of potential allergens and are observed to see if any changes happen.

'I had really bad hay fever and as results from other tests weren't clear, I had a nasal challenge test. It turns out that I am allergic to house dust mites, not pollen – so staying indoors in the pollen season just made things worse!' (Lydia, aged 15)

- Oral challenge test (for food allergies): Carefully measured increasing doses of the suspected food are given, while the person is observed for allergy symptoms.

Other allergy tests

Some people claim that they can work out the substances you are allergic to, using tests such as hair analysis or kinetic energy analysis. Beware of these tests, as there is no evidence that they are able to diagnose allergies. The only reliable tests at the present time are those performed at medically recognized allergy clinics.

Keeping the immune system healthy

The number of people suffering from allergies is growing, particularly in richer societies. A study in 1999 found that 38 per cent of Americans were affected by allergy. It is thought that the increase is due to differences in the environment in developed countries. One issue is that of increasing cleanliness. Some people think that our immune system may need to be exposed to regular small doses of dirt and disease in order to give it a work-out and keep it healthy. In rich countries, people tend to live in super-clean environments and children are less likely to play outside, and so their immune systems may not get the challenges they need to develop properly. Undeveloped immune systems are thought to be more likely to make the mistakes that cause allergies. Some researchers are even working to develop microbe vaccines that would exercise our immune systems without making us ill.

2 Allergic illnesses
Sneezes, wheezes and other discomforts

There are many different types of allergic illnesses. This chapter describes how they affect people, and also looks at some of the factors that increase a person's chances of experiencing such an illness. We will go on to investigate the substances that provoke allergic illnesses in Chapter 3.

Asthma

Asthma is a disease that affects the airways in your lungs. People who have asthma have very sensitive airways, which tend to become inflamed (red and swollen) and therefore narrow. When this happens, it is called an asthma attack. Anything that irritates the airways, making them inflamed and narrow and effectively starting an asthma attack, is called a trigger. Not all asthma is triggered by an allergy. However, allergies to house dust mites, animal hair, pollen and moulds are very common asthma triggers, particularly for young people.

A happy bunny?
Allergies to pet dander can trigger asthma.

Asthma attacks

When they become red and swollen, the airways become narrower. This makes it more difficult to get air in and out of the lungs, and so the person becomes breathless: they breathe faster in order to get enough oxygen into their body. It takes a lot of effort to get air in and out through narrow airways and the force needed can result in a whistling noise called a wheeze.

Normal airway

Inflamed airway

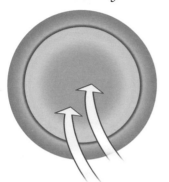

Airways
In an asthma attack, the airways in the lungs become inflamed, making it difficult for air to flow through.

Inflamed areas of the body produce fluid, as part of the immune system response. Inflamed lungs produce fluid called mucus, to try to flush out the irritant. This results in the asthma sufferer coughing, as they try to clear the mucus from their lungs in order to be able to breathe properly. It is very difficult to cough up mucus properly if your airways are narrow and inflamed. This means that asthma sufferers are caught between trying to cough up mucus and trying to breathe in and out to get enough oxygen into their systems. Experiencing an asthma attack can make the person feel frightened and anxious. This fear and anxiety can also cause breathlessness and can cause the airways to close up even more. Asthma attacks can be dangerous; sometimes they can be fatal. So they need prompt medical attention.

Asthma attacks vary in how often they occur, as well as in how bad they are. Some people with asthma experience them only occasionally, but people with severe allergy-induced asthma tend to experience the symptoms regularly. However, a main feature of asthma is that it is reversible: the symptoms disappear once the trigger is removed or once treatment is given. The long-term outlook for people with well-controlled asthma is good. People with allergy-induced asthma usually need to carry properly prescribed medicine, to soothe their airways and open them up, making it easier to breathe.

A growing problem

Asthma is a growing problem for countries around the world. The Global Initiative for Asthma estimates that approximately 150 million people worldwide suffer from asthma. In 1997, 1584 people died from asthma in the UK alone. More than a third of these were people below the age of 65. Asthma also has a substantial cost in time lost at work and school, not to mention the distress of asthma itself.

Allergic skin diseases

Allergic skin disease can vary in severity from small dry, hot, itchy patches of skin to conditions where nearly every skin surface is covered in a scaly, raw, bleeding, itchy rash. Although it can look unpleasant, allergic skin disease is not infectious. It is caused by an allergy to specific allergens.

Allergic skin conditions are a growing problem, particularly in the Western world. In the USA it is estimated that 1 in 9 people have an allergy-related skin condition, resulting in more than 7 million visits to health care providers each year.

There are several forms of allergic skin disease:

Atopic eczema

This is the most common form of eczema and affects people of all ages. 'Atopic' means that it is caused by an allergic reaction to an allergen. Common causes include house dust mites, pet hair, pollen and certain foods.

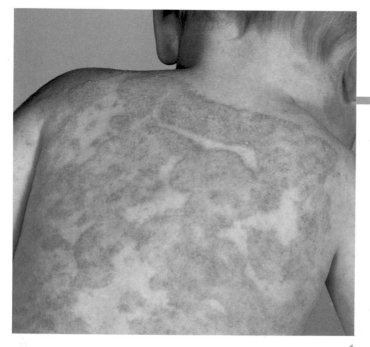

Eczema
Atopic eczema is caused by an allergy and can be very uncomfortable.

Atopic eczema is particularly itchy, and can be almost unbearable. Your skin becomes very dry, red and inflamed. Scratching (which can even occur in your sleep) can lead to your skin splitting and result in infection. Infected eczema can crack and weep (leak a clear fluid), and this is sometimes described as 'wet eczema'.

'I had bad eczema as a child. I remember the itching even now. But what I remember most is other children not wanting to hold my hand because they thought (wrongly) that they could catch something.'
(Toby, aged 42)

Atopic eczema commonly affects children. In the UK, up to 20 per cent of all children of school age have eczema and approximately 8 per cent of adults. In the USA, up to 9 per cent of the population are affected by allergic skin conditions. Most (but not all) people find that their eczema gradually improves as they get older. Two thirds of children with eczema find that it has virtually disappeared by the time they reach their mid-teens.

Allergic contact dermatitis

This skin condition occurs when an allergy develops to a substance that is in contact with your skin. It is commonly linked to nickel, which is often found in costume jewellery, buttons and buckles. It can also be caused by allergy to perfume or latex (rubber). At the point of contact with the allergen, your skin may become itchy, red and swollen, and small fluid-filled blisters may appear. These often break and dry out to leave crusts and scales. Eventually your skin may darken and become leathery.

'I developed an allergy to the metal in my watch. It was horrible. My skin got all red and scaly. It was so embarrassing. It went away eventually, after I left off the watch.'
(Alison, aged 17)

Urticaria or hives

Urticaria or 'hives' is a red itchy rash, with no blisters. This can be caused by a variety of things, including allergens. The rash can appear with more serious allergy problems, such as anaphylaxis, but it can also occur as a mild allergic response to things like eating strawberries or eggs. Health care workers may get urticaria from an allergy to latex gloves. Urticaria can also occur as the first sign of an allergy to medicines.

Hay fever (allergic rhinitis)

Allergic rhinitis causes sneezing, itching and watery eyes, runny nose and tiredness. It can be caused by an allergic reaction to several allergens, particularly pollens but also house dust mites, pet hair or moulds. Allergic rhinitis that only occurs at specific times of year is usually caused by pollen or moulds; problems that occur year round (sometimes called perennial rhinitis) may be caused by a pet hair or house dust mite allergy. Allergic rhinitis isn't usually a serious condition, but it can cause misery and prolonged suffering for people affected by it.

Allergic rhinitis usually develops before a person reaches their twenties. Once you have developed the condition, it does not mean that you will have it for the rest of your life. Symptoms of allergic rhinitis due to pollen allergy tend to be worst during a person's mid-twenties and then gradually diminish as they get older. Most people will have very few symptoms of allergic rhinitis by the time they are in their forties.

Approximately 26 million Americans (10 per cent of the population) are thought to suffer from allergic rhinitis and its estimated cost to the USA in 1990 was over $1.8 billion. (This is the cost of health care and time off work.) A similar proportion of the UK population are affected by the condition.

Not just spring
The sneezing and itchy, watery eyes associated with hay fever (allergic rhinitis) can occur at any time of year.

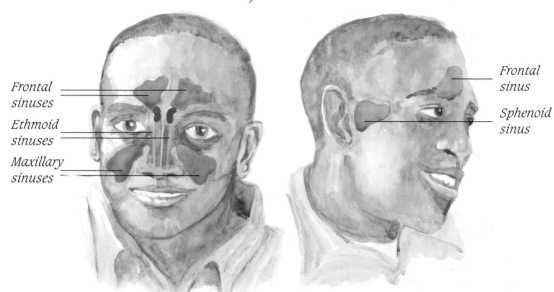

Frontal
sinuses

Ethmoid
sinuses

Maxillary
sinuses

Frontal
sinus

Sphenoid
sinus

Allergic sinusitis

Allergic sinusitis involves inflammation of the linings of
the sinuses. These are cavities that connect to your nose
and throat, and they help to moisten and warm the air you
breathe in, on its journey to your lungs. Allergic sinusitis
produces a clear, watery discharge from your nose, which
can run down the back of your throat and cause coughing.
Your nose may feel blocked and itchy. Your ears may also
feel itchy as a result of allergic sinusitis. You may sneeze

The sinuses
*Sinuses are cavities located
in the bones of your face
and forehead. They help
warm and moisten the air
that you breathe in.*

Understanding the problem

'We see many people with allergic sinus and allergic rhinitis conditions,
and these seem to us to be getting more common. The heaviest caseload
of people with the conditions occurs in spring and early summer, when the
pollen count is high. We are a rural practice, inland, away from sea
breezes, and we have quite a lot of downland and grassland around us.
We probably see more people with these allergic conditions than, say, a
practice near the coast, because of the geography of our area and the
types of plants that grow here. People can be dismissive of the importance
of these conditions because they are so common, but it is important to
take them seriously; they cause a lot of suffering, and not just in spring
and summer. Many people suffer all year round, due to allergies to house
dust mites and moulds.'
(Lionel, family doctor)

repeatedly and your eyes may water and itch. Common allergens that cause allergic sinusitis include pollen, pet hair, feathers and moulds.

Having allergic sinusitis makes you more likely to develop an infection in your sinuses and this can lead on to chronic sinusitis where the symptoms stay the same or worsen over many weeks or months. Chronic sinusitis is the most common chronic disease in the USA. In 1996, it was estimated to affect 12.6 per cent of the American population, which is about 38 million people, and to cost approximately $5.8 billion in health care expenses.

Allergic conjunctivitis

Allergic conjunctivitis is the name given to allergic reactions affecting the inner eyelid surfaces and membranes at the front of the eye called the cornea and conjunctiva. Both eyes are usually affected at the same time and you may experience intense itching, redness and inflammation of the tissues inside the eyelid. This form of allergic disorder usually occurs with allergic rhinitis or allergic sinusitis. It is often associated with sensitivity to house dust mite droppings, pollen and pet dander.

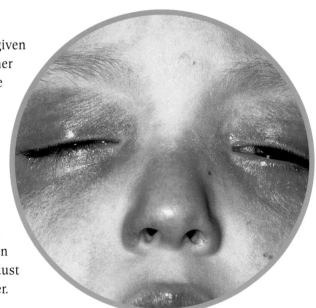

Allergic conjunctivitis
When you have allergic conjunctivitis, both eyes become itchy, swollen and red.

Food allergies

True food allergies are very rare. They can produce quite severe reactions in people who are susceptible to them. These reactions include swelling in the body (sometimes called oedema), swelling in the throat, urticaria (rash), vomiting, stomach cramps, diarrhoea and, in the most serious cases, anaphylaxis (see page 22). Food-related anaphylaxis is often associated with specific foods and occurs immediately or soon after the food is eaten. The food can cause a reaction even if it is present in minute amounts. This is particularly the case with nut allergies.

Rarely, food allergies can be connected to other allergic illnesses, such as allergic rhinitis and asthma. However, the symptoms then may not occur until several hours after the food has been eaten, and quite large amounts of the food need to be eaten for a reaction to occur.

'I'm allergic to milk. It's a right pain. I have to be really careful that I don't eat anything that has dairy products in it.'
(Ashley, aged 15)

Food allergies are most common in small children and babies whose immune systems are immature and therefore more likely to make the chemical mistake that causes them to react to a harmless substance. Most food allergies tend to lessen in severity as the individual gets older and their immune system matures. However, people with the most severe forms of food allergy, including allergies to peanuts, eggs and shellfish, tend to retain their allergy throughout their lives.

In the USA, food allergies are thought to affect approximately 8 per cent of children under 6 years old and 1 to 2 per cent of adults, and cause approximately 100 deaths per year. In the UK, food allergies are thought to affect approximately 5 per cent of children and, according to one survey, there were 8 deaths from food-related allergies between 1990 and 2000.

Food intolerance v Food allergy

There is an ongoing debate about the relationship between food allergies and food intolerance. Many people think that

Common allergens

Peanuts, tree nuts, wheat, soya, eggs, shellfish, fish and dairy products are the most common allergens in food allergies.

these two conditions are the same thing. They are not. Food allergy involves an adverse immune reaction to a particular food. Food intolerance involves an adverse reaction to food, which does not necessarily involve the immune system. Food intolerance can cause problems such as bloating, indigestion, tiredness, general aches and pains, headaches, diarrhoea and constipation. It cannot cause anaphylaxis (see below). Only a true allergy, which involves an immune system response, has the potential to cause an anaphylactic reaction.

'I thought I was allergic to milk but my doctor found that I wasn't. Apparently, I just have trouble digesting it. I'm not allergic to it. I am seeing a dietician now about improving my diet.'
(Leyla, aged 14)

If you experience any unpleasant symptoms that you think may be related to a food you have eaten, you need to get checked out by a medically qualified doctor. Food allergies can be very serious, occasionally fatal, and need to be taken seriously.

Anaphylactic shock

Anaphylaxis is the name given to the most severe form of allergic reaction. It is very rare and usually only a problem for people who are allergic to certain foods (such as milk, peanuts, shellfish, eggs and nuts), insect stings, latex (found in products such as rubber gloves and balloons), or some medicines (particularly those given by injection, in large doses). People most at risk of an anaphylactic reaction include those who have had an anaphylactic reaction before and people who have multiple allergies, especially those who have asthma plus food allergies.

In susceptible people, anaphylaxis can happen within five minutes or up to two hours after being exposed to the allergy-causing substance. Anaphylaxis involves a whole body response to an allergen. The person may find that their skin starts itching and a red rash may erupt over their body. Their lips may tingle and swell, and they may become hoarse and start to wheeze. Muscle cramping may occur. They get a sensation of tightness across the chest and they may feel short of breath and giddy. They may also feel confused and anxious. Sometimes they lose consciousness and, if not treated promptly, anaphylaxis can be fatal.

If someone does have a severe allergic reaction, it is important to get them to hospital fast. For information on what to do if someone has an anaphylactic reaction, see page 43. Often people who have this sort of severe allergy carry an injection of adrenalin with them. Adrenalin reverses the symptoms of anaphylaxis very quickly.

Some people have an anaphylactic reaction, appear to recover, and then the anaphylactic reaction returns two to three hours later. This form of response is called biphasic and can be particularly dangerous as it takes you by surprise.

Peanut panic

'My pal Abe's got a peanut allergy, I didn't think anything of it till he collapsed when we were at the roller park. Abe had a hotdog and the guy in the kiosk had been eating peanut butter sandwiches, then touched the hotdog. I've never seen anything like it! His lips got swollen and he got this rash, and then he sat down suddenly, holding his chest. His brother rushed up and stuck what looked like a pen in Abe's leg. It was an adrenalin injection. He came round a bit and they took him to hospital. I was sure glad his brother was there. I didn't have a clue.'
(Darius, aged 15)

Why allergic illnesses do or don't develop

The tendency to develop allergies is to some extent inherited through our genes. However, other factors also play a large part in determining whether you go on to develop allergic illnesses. These include the environment you live in, how many allergens you are exposed to, levels of stress, general health and whether you were breast-fed as a child.

Breast-feeding

Breast-feeding has been found to reduce the likelihood of a child developing an allergic disease, especially if it is continued for the first year of life. Babies don't only receive nutrients from breast milk but also antibodies, and this protects them from illness and helps their own immune systems to develop properly. Breast milk is easier for the baby to digest than cow's milk or soy milk. Also, the proteins in cow's milk and soy milk can produce allergies in children who are susceptible to them.

Breast milk
The antibodies and nutrients naturally present in breast milk help a baby's immune system to develop properly.

However, a mother breast-feeding a baby who is susceptible to allergic illnesses may have to be very careful what she eats, as there is some evidence that peanut allergens can be transmitted through breast milk to the baby. This would mean that a baby could become allergic to peanuts even if its only exposure to peanuts was through the mother eating them. This sort of sensitivity is thought to be very rare.

Virus infections

Virus infections including colds and flu are usually spread by coughing and sneezing. Coughs and sneezes distribute live viruses into the air, which you may breathe in if you are unlucky enough to be nearby. The viruses settle in your airways and multiply, irritating the airways and making you sneeze and cough so that you send more viruses out to infect other people. Your immune system notices it has an unwelcome visitor (or a few thousand) and sets to work to eradicate them before they can do major harm.

Any infection makes your immune system work harder. When your immune system is working hard, it is more likely to make a mistake that leads to an allergy developing. When your body is under stress (for example, from an illness), allergic illnesses tend to get more severe and you can become more sensitive to allergens. How this process works is unclear, but hopefully new research will help uncover the mechanisms behind it.

'My eczema gets much worse when I have a cold. It improves when I am fit and well.' (Anya, aged 16)

Stress and anxiety

Strong emotions have an effect on allergies. The link between what we feel and our health is very complex. Stress has been demonstrated to reduce the effectiveness of your immune system. For people who are at risk of allergies this can mean that their immune system is even more likely to make the mistake that causes an allergy to develop. So experiencing a stressful event such as the break-up of a relationship can reduce the effectiveness of your immune system and make it more likely that you will become ill or develop an allergy.

Environmental factors

High levels of air pollution make you more likely to develop allergies if you are genetically susceptible to them. Also, if you have an allergic illness, air pollution can make your symptoms worse because it irritates areas that are already inflamed. However, air pollution has not been proved to cause the development of allergies.

No smoking

Cigarette smoke is a common airborne pollutant that can make allergic illnesses worse. A baby born into a smoker's family is far more likely to develop allergies than a baby born into a non-smoking family.

3 Allergens Where they are found

Allergens are substances present in the environment that can cause an allergic response. An allergy occurs when a genetically susceptible person is exposed to a large enough quantity of allergen in their environment to provoke the development of an allergic reaction. How much allergen is enough to produce an allergic response depends on the individual and how sensitive they are. Many substances are potential allergens, and most of them occur naturally in the environment; very few are man-made. In this chapter, we will examine the most common allergens.

House dust mites

House dust mites are one of the most common allergens. These microscopic creatures, distant relatives of the spider, love our modern standards of living; they flourish in warm, humid conditions and live on the skin cells that we shed every day. The mites themselves do not cause allergies; it is their droppings that cause the problem. House dust mites produce up to 20 dung pellets a day. These contain partly digested skin cells (their favourite food) and enzymes, wrapped in a protein covering. (The enzymes continue to break down the remaining skin cells

Allergens at home
Allergens can be present in high levels in warm, humid, unventilated homes.

so that the mites can eat them again later and get some more nourishment from them.) It is the dung covering that is the main allergen.

House dust mites do not drink, but they contain up to 80 per cent water. This means that they need a humid, moist environment to survive. House dust mites live happily in warm (not too hot and not too cold), moist, unventilated homes: in bedding and soft furnishings, curtains, carpets, cushions, soft toys and anywhere dusty. There are millions of them even in the cleanest homes.

Dust mite
House dust mites are found in dust and in the soft furnishings of even the cleanest home. This coloured electron micrograph shows a dust mite on some fabric fibres.

Cockroaches

People who are allergic to house dust mite droppings may also be sensitive to cockroach allergens (see cross reactivity, page 33). Cockroach scales, eggs, saliva and droppings are all potent allergens, which are also found in house dust. Cockroaches eat almost anything, but their main food sources are waste food, paint, wallpaper paste and book bindings. Cockroaches also need water, warmth and a place to live (cracks and crevices). Cockroaches are a big problem in many countries across the world, particularly those with warmer climates.

Pet hair and feathers

Pets are a common source of allergens. It is possible to develop allergies to hair, skin scales (dander), saliva, urine and faeces of animals and birds. Any home with a pet will be full of these microscopic particles, especially in soft furnishings. It is difficult to get rid of these allergens. Dander from pets can still cause a problem up to six months after the pet has left the house. Research published in June 2001 from the USA found that more than 330,000 cases of asthma in children could be directly related to having a pet in the household.

Medicines

Medicines are important tools for fighting disease and only rarely cause allergies. However, the reactions can be severe. Some people can have anaphylactic reactions to some medication. If you are sensitive to certain medicines it is important that everyone involved in your medical care is aware of this. Most allergies to medication first show when a rash develops after taking the drug. People with asthma may find that they have an asthma attack after taking a medicine. Any reaction of this sort should be reported to your doctor immediately.

Some medicines are more likely to cause an allergic response than others. These include penicillin, aspirin, non-steroidal anti-inflammatory drugs and any drug that is given intravenously (directly into a vein) and in large doses.

Household chemicals

Many common household cleaners contain chemicals called volatile organic compounds, which can trigger allergies. These are chemicals made from oil and petroleum and can cause irritation to eyes, nose, lungs and skin as well as allergic reactions. Other products that contain these chemicals and can trigger allergies include air fresheners, paints, glues, varnishes and some aerosol sprays.

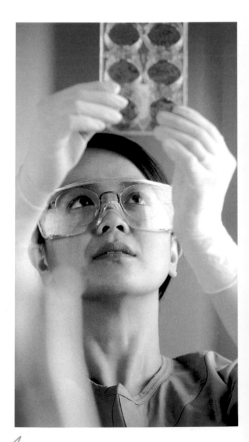

Researching detergents

'We have to be aware of the potential of the new detergents we are working on to cause allergies. Many of them are irritants, which can cause skin problems anyway. People should always wear gloves when using household cleaning products. I myself have asthma and I have to be very careful to take precautions when I am working with cleaning products. For some experiments I wear a respirator, to ensure that I don't breathe in the fumes.'
(Ling, chemist researching new detergents)

Natural gas and kerosene

The gases given off by natural gas and kerosene cookers and heaters are not allergens, but they do increase the potency of other allergens. It is thought that the gas binds to the allergen particles and makes it more likely that the immune system will react to the particle and start an allergy. One study found that cooking with kerosene increased your risk of developing an allergic illness by 78 per cent.

Food

It is possible to be allergic to any food, but up to 90 per cent of all food allergies are caused by eight groups. They are: milk, eggs, soy, wheat, peanuts, tree nuts (cashew nuts, hazelnuts, walnuts, etc), shellfish and fish. Food allergies can cause a range of allergic problems, such as hives, rhinitis, asthma and eczema. They can also be responsible for the most severe form of allergic response, anaphylaxis.

Peanuts are the food most commonly linked with anaphylaxis (though other food allergies can also result in anaphylaxis). Once an anaphylactic response to a food has been started, even the tiniest trace of the food can provoke the response. For people with peanut sensitivity, this can mean that they have to be careful about eating any foods that have been produced in a factory or kitchen where peanuts have been used, even if the foods themselves do not contain peanut products. It can also mean being aware of the contents of cosmetics. Arachis oil, which is derived from peanuts, has excellent skin-softening properties and, in the past, was frequently used in cosmetics.

Nut allergies
Peanuts are a well-known cause of food allergies, but tree nuts such as cashews, brazils and walnuts can have the same effects.

It is essential that anyone with severe forms of food allergy keeps emergency treatment with them (see Chapter 4, page 42).

Moulds

Mould spores can trigger an allergic reaction in some people, causing perennial rhinitis or asthma. Moulds are an essential part of the ecosystem; they help to break down plant and animal material into vital nutrients needed by other plants. Mould spores are like seeds from a plant: they enable the moulds to reproduce themselves. They are released into the air, usually during late summer and autumn, a time when you often see their fruiting bodies – fungi and mushrooms. However, moulds that grow indoors can release their spores at any time of year.

Mould spores can be found in warm or cool moist places, indoors or outside. Our well-insulated warm houses are prime breeding grounds for moulds. They thrive on windows prone to condensation, in damp areas around sinks, in bathrooms and in damp walls and roofs. Moulds also live in the compost around pot plants. Their spores often collect in house dust.

Pollen

Pollen is a powerful allergen and is linked to several allergic illnesses, particularly perennial rhinitis and asthma. There are many varieties of pollen. Some people are sensitive to just one and so will experience more allergic symptoms when that particular pollen is in the air. Others are sensitive to several different pollens and their symptoms will be more long-lasting. Some pollens are more likely to provoke an allergic response than

Pollen timetable
Different types of plant produce pollen at different times of the year. If you have hay fever, you can sometimes work out which pollens you are sensitive to by keeping a record of when your symptoms are worst.

Spring – tree pollen

Late spring to mid-summer – grass pollen

Mid-summer to early autumn – weed pollen

others. Grass pollens are particularly bad, as are the pollens of oil-seed rape and ragweed. Oil-seed rape has become an increasing problem across Europe, where it is grown for oil and as a food crop for animals.

Pollen is such a powerful allergen that it has been found that children born during the pollen season are more likely to develop asthma. When babies are born, their immune systems are immature and they are vulnerable to infection. Because of this, they are also vulnerable to develop allergies if they are genetically susceptible. Recent research has highlighted the importance of reducing the number of allergens that babies are exposed to, in order to reduce the likelihood of them developing allergic diseases.

'When I get stung by a wasp, I get bad swelling and feel terrible. Anti-histamines help. I tend to carry them with me in the wasp season.'
(Toby, aged 17)

Stinging insects

Allergies to insect stings can be very dangerous. This form of allergy causes at least 40 deaths per year in the USA and affects approximately 3.3 per cent of the population. The most common stinging insects include wasps, bumble bees, honey bees, hornets and, in the USA, yellow jackets, fire ants and harvester ants.

Wasp stings
Some people are allergic to insect stings. These allergies can cause severe swelling and sometimes anaphylaxis.

The most common allergic reaction to insect stings involves swelling of the area stung, larger than the site of the sting. For example, if you are stung on the foot, an allergic reaction might cause your whole foot – or even your leg and foot – to swell. You may also experience a fever and feel sick. If someone is severely allergic to insect stings, anaphylaxis can happen within minutes of receiving the sting. It is essential that anyone susceptible to this form of allergy carry emergency medication with them (see Chapter 4, page 42).

Allergens in the workplace

Working environments often bring us into contact with potential allergens. These can cause allergies to develop in people who are susceptible to them but have never had any symptoms before. Allergies caused by allergens in the workplace are called occupational allergies. The majority of occupational allergies cause asthma or dermatitis (skin allergy).

Trying to find the cause of an occupational allergy can be tricky. One study found that, of an estimated 6 million chemicals in the environment, approximately 2,800 could be classed as allergenic. Some substances in the workplace are well-known allergens. These include:

- isocyanates: these are chemicals often used in spray-painting, adhesives, foams, paints and plastics;
- fumes from soldering and welding, processes often used in the electronics industry;
- organochemicals found in some floor cleaners;
- dust, especially from grains (including flour), wood dust (especially hard woods and western red cedar) and latex dust;
- latex.

Latex

Latex is produced from the sap of the *Hevea Brasiliensis* tree and has been used extensively in manufacturing, particularly for making tyres, condom contraceptives, balloons, tubing, flooring, shoes and – since 1888 – surgical rubber gloves. It is an extremely useful substance but, unfortunately, it is also a particularly potent allergen. Latex allergy can cause eye problems, sneezing and coughing, hives

'I developed an allergy to the hair dye chemicals we use. We were supposed to wear gloves to prevent this, but sometimes I didn't. I wish I had listened now.'
(Denise, hair stylist)

Surgical gloves
Health care workers who become allergic to latex gloves need to use surgical gloves that do not contain this substance.

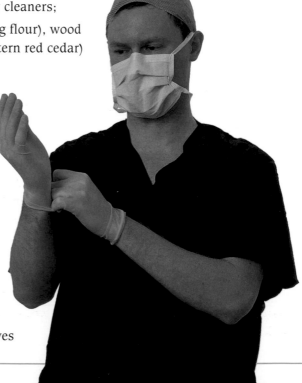

and occasionally anaphylaxis. In the USA, latex is responsible for approximately 220 cases of anaphylaxis and 3 deaths per year.

Latex allergies are a particular problem for:

- health care workers who wear latex gloves;
- food handlers (who also wear latex gloves);
- workers in manufacturing industries using latex products.

However, latex allergies do not only affect people at work, as rubber products are everywhere. Latex is even used to coat glossy paper. Latex can be found in elasticated clothing, footwear, condoms and diaphragms, rubber bands, toys, nappies, magazines; the list is huge. Sufferers from a latex allergy can also be at risk from food that has been packed by people wearing latex gloves.

Latex allergies and spina bifida

Latex allergies are a particular issue for people with spina bifida, a condition that occurs when the spinal bones do not form properly when a baby is developing in the womb. It now seems that up to 78 per cent of people with spina bifida may have latex allergy. Why this should be is not clear, but one theory is that people with spina bifida have constant exposure to latex products from a very early age, through surgery, diagnostic tests and various other medical procedures, and that this might increase their susceptibility to the allergy.

Cross reactivity

Sometimes an allergic reaction is caused by a substance that is chemically very similar to the allergen that first provoked the allergy. This is called cross reactivity and is an important issue for people who suffer from allergies. Substances that are alike in their chemical construction do not necessarily look or taste alike, and so some unexpected, unrelated things might trigger the usual allergic response. For example, people with latex allergies may well have cross-reactivity allergies to bananas, avocados and chestnuts, because proteins in these foods are very similar in chemical structure to the latex protein. Similarly, people with an allergy to house dust mites may show cross reactivity to storage mites, bird feathers, egg yolks and shrimp proteins.

4 Treating allergies
Soothing and preventative medicines

Treating asthma

Treatment for asthma involves reducing exposure to asthma allergens and regularly taking the medication prescribed by the doctor. People with asthma often require more than one type of treatment and so their doctor and asthma nurse help put together a treatment plan that is right for the individual person.

Relievers

Relievers are usually prescribed as inhalers, although there are also some reliever tablets. Inhalers are a form of medicine that you breathe directly into your airways so that it starts to work immediately at the site of the problem. Relievers work by making the muscles relax around the inflamed, narrow airways. This enables the airways to open further, making it easier to breathe.

Preventers

Preventers are also usually taken as inhalers. They work by soothing the lining of the airways. They reduce inflammation and make the airways less sensitive to allergens. When you take preventers properly, you are less likely to experience a severe asthma attack. For preventers to work effectively, you have to take them every day, even if you feel well, and it can take up to 14 days for them to start taking effect.

Inhalers
The inhaler in this picture is being used with a spacer. Spacers enable the medicine to be breathed in effectively, so none of it is lost.

'The inhalers help as long as I take them regularly.'
(Isabella, aged 15)

Inhaled steroids are one main type of preventer. They are a very effective preventative treatment for allergic asthma. The steroids mimic chemicals that are naturally produced in the body and which soothe inflammation and irritation. Inhaling the steroid medicine, taking it straight to the inflamed airways, means that only tiny amounts are needed and there are few side effects.

'I've had asthma since I was small. It's better than it used to be. I try not to let it rule my life.'
(Simeon, aged 16)

Another type of preventer inhaler is called a mast cell stabilizer or inhibitor. Mast cells are part of the immune system (see page 8). Once sensitized, they react to the presence of allergens by releasing the chemical histamine into your bloodstream. Mast cell stabilizer medicines calm down the mast cells and stop them being so active. This reduces the inflammation in your airways and makes them less sensitive to any allergens you breathe in.

Some other preventer medicines are antileukotrines. These are taken as tablets. Leukotrines are chemicals found in the muscles around your airways and in the lining of your lungs. They make these muscles irritable (twitchy) and cause them to grow larger. Antileukotrine medication works against this process, making it easier to breathe. Antileukotrines are a new component of asthma treatment and are becoming increasingly popular.

Antibiotics

People with asthma are at a higher than normal risk of developing chest infections. Antibiotics are an effective treatment for chest infections caused by bacteria.

Some people may have an allergic reaction to an antibiotic, particularly penicillin, and develop an itchy rash and swelling around the face and lips. If this happens to you, you should stop taking the antibiotic and contact your doctor for advice.

Steroid tablets

Occasionally people with asthma find that their symptoms get worse. At these times, their doctor may prescribe steroid tablets. These are a much stronger dose than a steroid inhaler and are very effective at reducing airway inflammation. Usually the steroid tablets only need to be taken for 3 to 14 days.

Treating allergic rhinitis (including hay fever)

As with most allergies, allergic rhinitis is treated by a mixture of avoiding the allergen and taking medication to relieve the symptoms. The medication can be divided into three main sections:

Antihistamines

Histamines are chemicals that are produced by the immune system and cause inflammation. Antihistamines are medicines that stop the inflammation process. They can be taken as tablets, nasal sprays or eye drops, in order to relieve the symptoms of allergy at the point where they are most irritating.

Antihistamines are available over the counter at pharmacies, and qualified pharmacists are able to give information about which type is most appropriate. However, it is essential that you are careful about the mixture of medication you are taking for your allergies, as taking more than one type of medication, such as an antihistamine with certain cough preparations, can cause dangerous side effects. Medical advice should always be sought about taking a variety of medicines, to ensure that they do not interact and cause you harm.

'The antihistamine I used to take for hay fever made me feel really sleepy. Then mum talked to the pharmacist and found one that helps stop my eyes watering but doesn't make me sleepy. Much better!'
(Harry, aged 14)

Decongestants

These reduce the symptoms of nasal congestion that often accompany rhinitis problems. Decongestants must only be used for a few days at a time. If used for longer, they can lose their effectiveness and cause rebound nasal congestion when they are stopped. As with antihistamines, it's wise to ask the pharmacist about which would be suitable and how to use the treatment.

Preventative treatment

Preventative medicines for allergic rhinitis include mast cell inhibitors (see page 35) and steroids, which are also useful for reducing irritation. The amount of steroid needed to act as a preventer for allergic rhinitis is so small that there are rarely any side effects associated with its use. These preventers are usually given in the form of nasal sprays, nose drops or eye drops.

If these forms of treatment provide only limited relief, your doctor may suggest desensitization (see page 40).

Treating allergic sinusitis

Treatment for allergic sinusitis is very similar to that for allergic rhinitis: based on avoiding the allergens that produce symptoms and treating any symptoms that do occur with antihistamines and preventer medication such as mast cell stabilizers and steroids. You may also need to take medication to relieve the pain caused by congested sinuses. Your doctor may recommend that you use saline (salty water) nasal spray or rinses, in order to reduce the feeling of pressure from blocked sinuses.

Treating allergic conjunctivitis

Treatment for allergic conjunctivitis also involves the use of antihistamines, mast cell stabilizers and steroids, in order to reduce the symptoms of allergy. For eye conditions, though, these are usually applied as eye drops, ointment or cream. For certain types of allergic conjunctivitis, especially a variety called atopic keratoconjunctivitis, which also affects the eyelid, cold compresses can help relieve the intense itching and swelling.

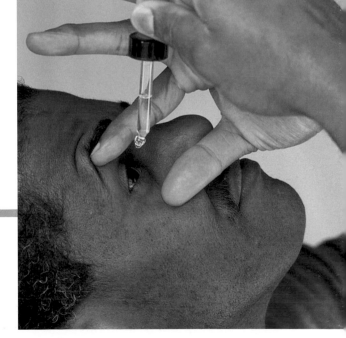

Eye relief
Antihistamine treatment can relieve the discomfort of allergic conjunctivitis.

Treating eczema and allergic contact dermatitis

There are several treatments for eczema and allergic contact dermatitis, which can be very effective when they are used as part of a regime that also involves avoiding allergens.

Emollients

Emollients are creams that reduce water loss from the skin and prevent dryness and the itch associated with dry skin. The emollients provide a barrier between the skin and anything that might irritate it. They come in various forms: ointment, cream and lotion. Some emollients are used instead of soap. Others are applied as often as required to prevent the skin becoming dry. There are many emollients available and it is worth trying a few, as it is possible to become allergic to substances in an emollient.

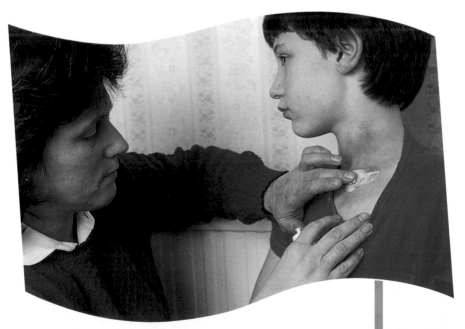

Steroid creams

Doctors sometimes prescribe steroid creams to treat eczema and allergic contact dermatitis that is very inflamed and uncomfortable. Steroid creams lessen the inflammation and irritation of a skin rash and can help the

Applying cream
You need to wash your hands after applying steroid creams in order to prevent them coming into contact with your eyes or mouth.

healing process by reducing the production of histamine (see pages 8-9). Steroid creams come in many different strengths and your doctor will prescribe the lowest dose necessary to help relieve your skin condition. Steroid creams are applied in a very thin layer to the affected area. It is important to use as little as possible, as the medication is very strong.

Other treatments

Other treatments for allergic skin conditions include antihistamine tablets or creams, ultraviolet light treatment (only usually used for severe eczema), and wet-wrap bandaging to reduce itching. It can also help to keep cool, especially at night, and to make sure that fingernails are kept short to reduce the damage done by scratching. Sometimes it is recommended that children wear cotton mittens at night, to stop them scratching in their sleep.

'My daughter had eczema as a baby. We used to have to put mittens on her at night to stop her scratching. Poor little mite.'
(Jean, aged 30)

Treating urticaria and hives

Antihistamines are the main medication used to treat urticaria. They can help relieve any itchiness accompanying the rash and help the rash to gradually get better. If the condition does not improve, a doctor may prescribe steroid creams or (rarely) steroid tablets. Allergic urticaria usually disappears within a few days if you avoid the allergen that causes the rash to occur.

If you get hives after you have eaten something or been stung, then it is important that you visit your doctor, as it can be a sign that you are developing a serious allergy that may result in anaphylaxis.

Steroid tablets

Very occasionally, with severe allergic skin conditions, it may be necessary to take steroid tablets. Again, the doctor will prescribe the lowest dose possible. If steroid tablets are taken for a long time, there is a risk of side effects. These include growth retardation (mainly a problem for children who are still growing), developing a round (moon) face, weight gain (due to an increase in appetite), bruising and osteoporosis.

People who take steroids need to carry a steroid card with them, so that if they have an accident the doctor treating them will know they are on steroids and that they need to keep taking them. Steroids are very powerful and need to be reduced slowly.

Treating food allergies

The only effective treatments for food allergies are an exclusion diet (excluding the allergens that cause your symptoms) and sometimes desensitization. However, the latter is usually considered too dangerous for people at risk of anaphylaxis.

You should always consult a doctor before starting an exclusion diet, as it is vital to ensure that you still get all the nutrients you need. It can also be very difficult to follow such a diet. We eat so many convenience foods and packaged foods, and there may be allergens 'hidden' in the ingredients of all of these. People with food allergies have to become experts at reading food labels. (The issue of avoiding food allergens is covered in more detail in Chapter 5.)

The risk of cross-contamination is a problem too. Cafés, restaurants and food-processing plants often deal with very many different foods and it is impossible to guarantee that traces of one food are not carried on to another. Such cross-contamination could be very serious. For some people it takes only a few molecules of a food substance to set off an allergic reaction. People at risk of an anaphylactic reaction to a food allergy should carry an emergency adrenalin injection with them, in case they come across the food allergen unexpectedly.

Food awareness
People with food allergies have to read the list of ingredients on each package very carefully, to make sure that they avoid the foods they are allergic to.

Desensitization

If you have an allergy, it may be possible to have desensitization treatment at an allergy clinic. This involves being given a series of injections over several months.

The treatment begins with skin prick testing (see page 10), to confirm what you are allergic to (the allergen). This is followed by a series of tiny injections containing minute amounts of the allergen. The injections may be continued for a long time: depending on the individual, they can be given over a period of several months up to five years. The aim of the injections is to retrain your immune system not to react to the allergen. It is important to try to avoid the allergen while you are having the desensitization injections.

Desensitization can be very effective at reducing the severity of allergy-induced illness and, if you react well to the treatment, improvement in symptoms can last for several years after finishing the injection course. There is a small possibility of having an anaphylactic reaction to desensitization injections. Therefore, a competent medical practitioner with emergency equipment available should always perform the treatments. In practice, this usually means it is best to have the treatment in a hospital allergy clinic.

Working at the allergy clinic

'I work in an allergy clinic attached to our local hospital. We see a large number of people every day with various allergies. Desensitization is one of the treatments we use. For example, if you had severe hay fever and it affected your school work or stopped you working, then your doctor may decide that desensitization would be an appropriate treatment. It doesn't take long to come in and have the injections, but you do have to come in regularly for many months. We have to be sure that people are going to keep coming, as the treatments are expensive and, if you miss a few, then you might as well not have had any. For people who do have the whole course it seems to be pretty effective. I'd say that the majority of patients here find their symptoms improve.'
(Andrew, allergy clinic nurse)

Emergency treatment for asthma

Occasionally, someone with asthma may have a severe asthma attack, which does not respond to the reliever medicine they keep with them. If an asthma attack does not improve after a dose of reliever medicine, you should contact your doctor or call an ambulance (or get someone to do this for you) and keep taking your reliever medicine every few minutes until the ambulance arrives or the doctor directs you to do otherwise. Don't be afraid of causing a fuss, even at night.

In hospital, you may be given some oxygen to help your breathing. You may also be given a nebulizer with a high dose of reliever medication. (A nebulizer is a machine that pumps air through a mixture of medicine and saline in order to create a fine mist.) You may be given steroids and, if you have a chest infection, you may also be given antibiotics. You may need to stay in hospital until your asthma is under control again.

Emergency treatment for anaphylaxis

Anaphylaxis can happen within five minutes of being exposed to an allergen. The reaction involves the whole body: an itchy red rash may develop, lips may tingle and swell, the throat may become swollen so that the voice becomes hoarse, breathing becomes difficult so the person may wheeze, muscle cramps may occur and the person feels dizzy, confused and anxious.

Emergency injection
People who are at risk of anaphylaxis often carry an emergency injection of adrenalin with them.

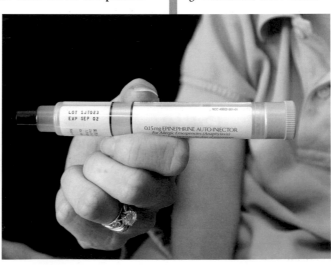

If someone has an anaphylactic reaction, it is essential that they have an emergency injection of adrenalin. If the person has an emergency shot with them, they should use it immediately. It is also vital to get the person to hospital as

Anaphylaxis first aid

If someone is having an anaphylactic reaction:

1 Ask if they carry an emergency adrenalin shot. If they do, remind them to use it.
2 Call an ambulance. It is important to get them to hospital as quickly as possible. (Do not allow them to drive themselves to hospital.)
3 Keep them sitting up as this makes breathing easier.
4 Reassure them and keep them calm.
5 Do not give them anything to eat or drink.
6 If they carry a reliever inhaler, they may take a puff.
7 If they become drowsy or unconscious, put them in the recovery position.
8 Keep a careful watch on their breathing and pulse. Be prepared to use mouth-to-mouth resuscitation if necessary.

quickly as possible so that they can be given an adrenalin injection, and so that their essential body systems can be supported if the reaction continues.

Adrenalin (also called epinephrine) is a natural hormone produced by the body. It reverses the anaphylactic reaction by increasing blood pressure and reducing swelling. People known to be at risk of anaphylactic reactions usually carry a dose of adrenalin with them, in the form of a 'pen' or automatic injector. It is essential to get an injection of adrenalin as soon as the symptoms of anaphylaxis start; the sooner it is given, the less likely the reaction will be severe.

Anaphylaxis can be fatal so, if you are at risk, it is essential to carry an adrenalin shot with you everywhere. You never know when you might come across the allergen that causes the reaction. It is also wise to wear a Medicalert® bracelet or necklace that gives details of your condition, and to make sure that the people you are with know what symptoms to look out for and what to do in an emergency.

Recovery position

This is the safest position for someone who is unconscious, while waiting for emergency help. Ensure that their chin is up, to keep their airway open so that they can breathe.

Complementary therapies

No complementary therapy can cure allergies, but some can help people manage them better and reduce their symptoms. If you want to try a complementary therapy, do not stop taking your prescribed medicine and let your doctor know before you begin. This is important, as some complementary medicines can be harmful for people with allergies.

Exercise

Exercise-based therapies, such as yoga, Pilates, T'ai chi and martial arts, can all have a beneficial effect on allergic asthma symptoms. This is because they increase your general fitness level and they all involve breathing exercises, which can help you stay in control during an asthma attack. Another potential benefit from these exercise therapies is that they involve learning to relax. This can be useful in preventing asthma attacks from becoming severe, by helping to keep you calm and relaxed when an attack occurs.

Acupuncture

Acupuncture involves the insertion of very thin needles at points on your body, based on Chinese theories of natural energy paths. Some research into the benefit of acupuncture for people with asthma and allergic rhinitis has shown that it can be helpful in the short term. Acupuncture does not normally produce side effects. However, it is wise to make sure that you are seeing a properly qualified practitioner who is using sterile acupuncture needles.

Pilates training
Exercise classes help improve your fitness and your breathing technique, and this can help you stay in control during an asthma attack.

Homeopathy

A homeopathist makes a detailed assessment of a person's problem and character and then treats the problem with tablets containing a very tiny amount of a substance that would produce similar symptoms if taken in large doses. Homeopathy can be helpful if you know what you are allergic to. Some research has shown that some people with allergies can be helped by homeopathy – particularly by a form of treatment called homeopathic immunotherapy. However, more research is needed to prove the value of this.

Royal jelly and propolis

These products can provoke a severe allergic reaction in people who are allergic to pollen.

Complementary medicines

These include herbal medicine, Chinese herbal medicine and homeopathy. Some herbal medicines have been shown to help reduce asthma symptoms. Those that may be helpful include ginko biloba, tylophora asthmatica, coleus forskholii and saiboku-to. However, some herbal medicines can be harmful and you should always get your doctor's advice before taking a herbal preparation.

Some products from bees, particularly royal jelly and propolis, which are commonly sold as medicinal products, can be very dangerous for people with allergies. They can provoke a severe allergic reaction. It is wise to avoid any products containing royal jelly and propolis if you have asthma or allergies to pollen.

'Homeopathy was really helpful – when I took the remedy properly, my symptoms were a lot better.'
(Nicole, aged 24)

The medicines and treatments described in this chapter are one part of preventing allergic illnesses and relieving their symptoms. The second component of managing allergies successfully involves reducing your exposure to allergens. We will investigate this in Chapter 5.

5 Living with allergies
Risk reduction and being prepared

Just as important as taking the correct medication is identifying what you are allergic to and reducing your exposure to it. This can be harder than it sounds. If you are unsure what causes your allergy, and skin prick tests are not an option, then one way to try to find out is by keeping a diary recording your allergy symptoms and your contact with the common allergens. You may find that a pattern emerges. For example, your symptoms may be worse in the morning and improve during the day. This might indicate that you are sensitive to something in your bedroom, perhaps house dust mites. You could then take action to reduce your exposure and see if there is an improvement in your symptoms.

At home
Lots of soft furnishings, combined with central heating and poor ventilation, can cause a large build-up of house dust mites.

Reducing dust mite difficulties

The rise in the number of people across the world who suffer from allergies is closely associated with rising wealth and standards of living. In today's soft-furnished, centrally heated, double-glazed buildings, people are exposed to more allergens than at any time in history. One of the main allergens, which increase hugely under these conditions, are house dust mite droppings. House dust mites live on dead skin cells, which we shed every day. They like a warm, moist environment to live and breed in.

So what could you do to reduce the number of house dust mites – and their droppings – in your home? Here are some tips.

- If you can afford to, replace old, worn mattresses, pillows and duvets.
- Consider buying dust mite proof covers for your mattress and pillows.
- Change your bedclothes regularly (weekly, if possible) and wash the sheets at a high temperature setting.
- Make sure your bed is properly aired every day. Turn back the covers over the end of the bed and leave the bottom sheet open to the light and air for a few hours. Because house dust mites cannot drink, they rely on a humid dark environment to stay alive.
- Wash soft toys and then put them in a plastic bag in the freezer for a few hours. Cold temperatures kill dust mites.
- Cushions and pillows also benefit from a regular stay in the freezer (if you have one large enough).
- Use a vacuum cleaner with a special filter and damp dust regularly. (Some people who are very sensitive to dust mites need to do this every day.)
- Reduce the number of soft furnishings in your house. Use blinds instead of curtains. Replace carpets with hard flooring such as lino or wood.
- Make sure that any soft furnishings left are vacuumed and cleaned regularly.
- Make sure there is adequate ventilation. Open windows and air your house daily.

'My allergic rhinitis has improved a lot since we started getting rid of dust mites.'
(Rosa, aged 15)

'If my room is not dusted and vacuumed every day, my asthma gets worse.'
(Anka, aged 13)

Avoiding food allergens

If you have a food allergy, you may try to avoid the allergen responsible by excluding it from your diet. However, you should consult your doctor about following such a diet, as completely excluding one food source can be bad for your health. You need to ensure that you get all the nutrients required for good health and growth. If your doctor suspects that you have a food allergy, she or he may suggest that you talk to a dietician, who can help you make sure that you eat a balanced diet and keep as healthy as possible.

'Before I kiss someone, I have to ask them what they have been eating. Anaphylaxis can be a very disappointing way to finish an evening if I don't check.'
(Katlyn, aged 17)

Food allergens can be very difficult to avoid. You have to learn to read the labels on packaged food very carefully, as the same food substance can appear with different names on different packages. The following lists show some of the issues that people with food allergies need to bear in mind.

Milk allergies

- Shops often use the same surfaces and implements for serving dairy and other delicatessen products.
- Restaurants often put butter on steaks to add flavour.
- Some processed meats contain milk products.
- Some brands of canned tuna contain milk products.
- 'Casein' on food labels means that the food contains milk products.

Egg allergies

- Some vaccinations are grown in egg embryos and therefore may provoke an allergic reaction. The person should check with their doctor before having any vaccinations.
- Some egg substitutes contain real egg white.
- Many pasta products contain egg.
- Egg is used to create a foam topping on some drinks such as coffee or milkshakes.

Peanut and other nut allergies

- ⬡ Arachis oil is peanut oil.
- ⬡ Chocolate may be processed in factories that also process nuts.
- ⬡ Products from bakeries are often made in areas that also use nuts.
- ⬡ Sunflower seeds are often processed in equipment that is also used to process nuts.
- ⬡ Breakfast cereals are often processed in factories that also use nuts.
- ⬡ Natural or artificial flavouring may be derived from nuts.
- ⬡ Nuts may be one of the ingredients of products such as sauces, cereals, crackers, biscuits and ice cream, so labels need to be checked very carefully.
- ⬡ Bean bags, cushions and soft toys are sometimes filled with crushed nut shells.

Hard to choose
Choosing what to eat can be especially difficult for someone who needs to avoid food allergens.

Fish allergies

- ⬡ It is wise for someone allergic to one species of fish to avoid all species, because of the risk of cross reactivity (see Chapter 3, page 33).
- ⬡ Seafood restaurants or restaurants serving fish should be avoided because of the risk of cross contamination.
- ⬡ Fish protein can be present in the air, so fishmongers, docks and markets selling fish products should all be avoided.
- ⬡ Caesar salad dressing and Worcester sauce often contain fish paste.
- ⬡ Surimi (imitation crab meat) is often made from fish.

Soy allergies

⬤ Soybean products are used in the majority of processed foods around the world and particularly in the USA.

⬤ Soybean products are particularly found in bread and baked goods, canned tuna, cereal, crackers, biscuits, sauces, soups and sometimes peanut butter.

Wheat allergy

⬤ Many processed foods contain wheat products. Food labels should be read very carefully.

⬤ Some types of imitation crabmeat contain wheat.

Removing animal allergens

The allergens produced by furry and feathered pets are particularly hard to get rid of. If you have an allergy to animals, it is best not to have them at home at all. If you cannot live without them, make sure that they do not go into your bedroom and main living areas. You can also reduce the amount of dander produced by your pets by giving them a weekly bath, keeping them outside as much as possible and washing your hands after touching them. It is possible to remove pet allergens from your home by steam cleaning, but this is fairly drastic and expensive.

If you decide that your allergy is so severe that the pet has to go, then don't be surprised if your allergy symptoms do not improve immediately. It can take up to six months for pet hair and dander to disappear from a house completely.

Keeping cockroaches at bay

The parts of a cockroach that are most likely to cause allergic reactions are their saliva, outer coverings (cuticle), droppings and egg cases. Allergy to cockroaches can be severe and has been known to cause anaphylaxis.

Cockroach
Some people become allergic to cockroach saliva, shells, droppings or egg cases.

As big as mice

'I developed an allergy to cockroaches when we used to live in a flat. The flat was in an old block from the 1960s. It was damp and there was rubbish everywhere – no one looked after it – and the cockroaches! I swear that some of them were as big as mice. I've never seen anything like it. It was disgusting. I started to get a runny nose and itchy eyes and eventually they found out that I was allergic to cockroaches. But you couldn't get away from them in that dump. They were everywhere. We moved when Mum got a better job.'
(Morgan, aged 16)

It is important to avoid cockroaches as much as possible. Cockroaches need food, water, warmth and a place to hide in order to survive. To prevent them breeding in your home:

- Do not leave food out. Store it in airtight containers.
- Keep work surfaces, sinks, tables and floors clean. Clear all food crumbs and spilled food immediately.
- Wash dishes as soon as you have finished with them.
- Do not leave rubbish lying about indoors. Put it in containers with tight-fitting lids, and empty these daily into an outside bin. Keep newspapers, boxes and other rubbish outside, in sealed refuse containers.
- Repair any plumbing leaks or damp problems quickly.
- If you suspect a cockroach infestation, get professional help in dealing with it.

Taking care with household cleaners

Household cleaners contain a cocktail of chemicals, some of which can act as allergens and some of which are irritants and can produce symptoms very similar to an allergy, such as skin rashes and wheezing. Common chemicals in cleaning products that can become allergens include ammonia, chlorine, chloroform, isocyanates, isopropanol, perfume and solvents. To avoid contact with these chemicals, users should always wear household gloves. Also, remember that there are alternatives to modern household cleaners that are not as likely to cause an allergic reaction. These include:

- using a teaspoon of vinegar mixed with one litre of water for cleaning windows (newspaper is also good to use as a 'cloth' for cleaning windows);
- dissolving 1 teaspoon of bicarbonate of soda in water to clean fridges, freezers and sinks.

Choose cleaning products and washing powders labelled 'hypoallergenic'. This means 'not likely to act as an allergen'.

Getting rid of household moulds

Well-insulated, warm, humid homes are an ideal breeding ground for moulds. They thrive on windows prone to condensation, in kitchens and bathrooms. They also grow in damp plaster, wood and houseplant compost. For people who are allergic to moulds, the household kind are particularly troublesome because they release spores (the main allergen) throughout the year. The conditions loved by moulds are the same as those enjoyed by house dust mites and so many of the strategies to get rid of one of the problems also get rid of the other. To avoid or get rid of household moulds:

- Shut the bathroom door and open a window or use an extractor fan when running a bath or having a shower.
- Replace shower curtains regularly.
- Dry damp towels as quickly as possible.
- Dry clothes outdoors as much as possible and make sure that electric clothes dryers are vented outside.
- Make sure that rising damp or damp walls from defective guttering or roofing are dealt with quickly.
- Don't use potpourri as it can provide a growing surface for mould.

Mopping up
Condensation on windows is a prime breeding ground for moulds. The condensation needs to be removed every morning to prevent mould growing.

- Each day open windows so air flows through the home.
- Mop up condensation from windows daily.
- Clean the rubber around fridge and freezer doors, removing the black mould growth.
- Cut down on houseplants and regularly replace the top layer of soil where moulds grow.

Check your cooking fuel

Using domestic gas or kerosene for cooking can raise the level of nitrogen dioxide in your home and can result in increased sensitivity to allergens so that your allergy symptoms are more severe. Exposure to nitrogen dioxide is reduced if you keep kitchen windows and doors open while cooking and keep doors to the rest of the home shut. If you have severe allergies, it may be worth changing to another cooking fuel, such as electricity. Gas-fired central heating does not seem such a problem, as it is vented outside.

Managing a latex allergy

Latex allergies are quite difficult to manage, as you need to avoid a long list of products that contain latex. Around the home, for example, latex is found in elastic bands, clothing that contains elastic (e.g. knicker elastic, socks and some sportswear), ice cube trays, nappies, condoms, diaphragms, baby pacifiers and bottle teats, balls, balloons, cycle tyres and some decorating and art products. It is important to read the label of any product that is flexible or stretchy or may contain latex. Look for alternatives that contain silicone, plastic or vinyl.

It is also advisable to wear a Medicalert® bracelet or necklace. Medical procedures often involve products made with latex, such as medical gloves, bandages, catheters, intravenous tubing and tourniquets (used when taking blood). Even elastoplasts and adhesive tape can contain latex. If the doctor or hospital knows that you are allergic to latex, they can use alternative equipment that is safe for you.

Medicalert

Medicalert members wear a bracelet or necklace engraved with their allergy or illness, a personal ID number and the Medicalert phone number. In an emergency, doctors can contact Medicalert for complete medical information about the person that may affect their treatment.

PHONE UK: 020 7407 2318
ALLERGIC: LATEX
GB: 000000

Back

MEDIC ALERT

Front

Stinging insects: reduce your risk

An allergy to insect stings can be very serious, although, thankfully, this type of allergy is quite rare. Anaphylactic reactions to insect stings occur in less than 5 per cent of the people who are allergic to them.

Any insect sting that causes a skin reaction over 10 cm in size should be reported to your family doctor as you may be developing a sting allergy. If you are allergic to insect stings, there are several things you can do to minimize your chance of being stung:

- Use insect repellents when outside or inside during summer months, when stings are more likely.
- Don't wear clothing that attracts insects. This includes black, flowery or brightly coloured clothing and shiny surfaces.
- Wear shoes, to avoid being stung if you accidentally step on a stinging insect.
- Wear long sleeves and trousers.

Insect attractant
Avoid wearing brightly coloured loose clothing and eating sweet things outside if you are allergic to insect stings.

Moulds outside the home

Moulds outside are a vital part of the ecosystem, helping to break down organic matter and providing nutrients for other living things. They are commonly found in woodland, compost heaps, rubbish bins and tips – anywhere where there is dead plant or animal material. These moulds tend to produce spores in warm, moist conditions, so spring and autumn are more likely to be problematic for people allergic to moulds. Barns used for storing hay and grain are best avoided if you suffer from such an allergy.

- Avoid floaty clothes; close-fitting clothing makes it less likely that an insect will be trapped in the folds.

- Avoid strong perfumes and cosmetics with a powerful perfume.

- Avoid eating or drinking sweet things outside.

- Don't panic if you see an insect. Swatting at them and panicking make stings more likely. Keep still if a stinging insect lands on you; it will fly off quite quickly.

Pollen precautions

If your allergy is caused by pollen, it will be worse at certain times of the year. Pollen is very hard to avoid as it blows for many miles. Some areas tend to have a higher pollen count (a measure of the amount of pollen in the air) than others; in general, the pollen count tends to be less on the coast as sea breezes blow the pollen away. Regular reports on the current pollen count are published in local newspapers, on the internet, and on television and radio, to give you a guide as to when to take more precautions.

Pollen grains
This coloured electron micrograph shows pollen grains (pink) and dust (blue) on the surface of someone's trachea or windpipe.

- Wear sunglasses to prevent pollen irritating your eyes.

- Wear a pollen-resistant mask over your nose and mouth (you need to be quite courageous to go out like this).

- Wash your hair and shower every evening to remove any pollen grains that have attached themselves to you.

- Cover your bedclothes with a bedspread or sheet during the day to prevent pollen grains getting on your pillow.

- Damp dust daily to remove pollen grains that have got into the home.

- Vacuum daily using a bag that will filter out particles as small as pollen grains.
- Keep windows closed as much as possible during the pollen season.
- Keep pets outside as much as possible during the pollen season.
- Get someone else to mow the lawn and stay inside while it is being done.
- Avoid hanging washing out during the pollen season, as pollen grains may collect in it.
- Get a car with pollen filters.
- Avoid going out when pollen counts are high. (Levels are highest early in the morning, early evening, on windy days and during thunderstorms.)
- If you are severely affected it is possible to purchase high-powered air filters which will remove pollen grains from the air.

'One of the advantages of being allergic to pollen is that you get out of mowing the lawn (which I hate).'
(Jason, aged 12)

Allergies at work and school

Many working environments involve substances that are potential allergens. If someone's allergy symptoms are worse at work and improve when they are away from the workplace, they may have an occupational allergy. It can take many years for an occupational allergy to develop.

There is a great deal of legislation relating to the way allergenic substances are used in the workplace; in many countries, employers are obliged by law to ensure that workers are protected from exposure to allergens. Action to protect people from allergens at work can include installing proper ventilation, supplying equipment to prevent workers from being exposed to an allergen, and replacing an allergenic substance with an alternative. For example, if a worker's allergy is triggered by latex and the job involves wearing latex gloves, then the employer would be obliged to supply gloves made from a different substance.

School blues

Classes outside in the summer are not much fun if you have an allergy to pollen.

At school and college too, there are many substances that can act as allergens. Schools and colleges are usually covered by the same health and safety legislation that applies to working environments. If you are sensitive to a substance found at school – for example, wood shavings, chemical fumes, fur and feathers in biology, or chemicals used in art lessons – you need to let your teacher know. The school health and safety representative or medical personnel should be able to suggest alternatives to the substance you are sensitive to or ways of avoiding it.

Allergies can cause problems beyond just their symptoms for people at work and at school. If you suffer from an allergy, you may feel unwell and tired. This can result in days off sick and not performing at your best. Some people with allergies find that their school grades suffer. It is wise to let teachers and employers know about the problem, to reduce your exposure to allergens and to take appropriate medication to minimize the impact of your allergy.

'Allergies can be very difficult for some students to manage. Those with hay fever can find it really difficult to manage through exam time.'
(Astrid, school nurse)

Holidays

Holidays can be a mixed blessing for people with allergies. Some holiday destinations can be fantastic, especially if you are allergic to substances found in your normal home environment. The holiday gives you a break from unpleasant allergy symptoms. On the other hand, a holiday can be problematic if you go to a place that increases your exposure to the substances you are allergic to. For example, if you are allergic to pet hair and go to a holiday home that has had pets in it, then you may feel worse than at home. Or, if you are allergic to pollen and go to a countryside location during the pollen season, you could have a miserable holiday.

On holiday there is also the danger of coming across allergens unexpectedly. When you are in a new or unfamiliar environment, it can be far more difficult than it is at home to keep aware of the foods you are eating or the substances you come into contact with. For example, it may be more difficult to find out whether the food you are offered has been prepared in a place where nuts have been present.

Learning from experience

'I have bad eczema. I am allergic to perfumes and some detergents. It is very difficult for me if I come into contact with these things, as I get covered in a nasty rash that does not look pretty. It mostly affects my arms, but once, on holiday, I walked across the swimming pool floor with bare feet and I got eczema on the soles of my feet. They had been cleaning the floor, using a detergent I am allergic to. It was not nice. Now I wear jelly shoes in the swimming pool. The eczema is horrible but now I know what causes it, it is easier to avoid. The doctor has given me some special cream. When the rash is bad, I wear long sleeves so no one can see it. It is better than it used to be.'
(Stephanie, clerical assistant, aged 22)

These difficulties should not put you off holidays altogether. The important thing is to be well prepared. Make sure that people are aware of your allergy and the need to avoid the substances that cause problems. (This is particularly important for people with food, sting and latex allergies.) Always carry essential medication with you and ensure that you are prepared for emergencies. Be aware of situations that may bring you into contact with the substance that causes your allergy. Then, knowing that you are prepared in these ways, you can relax and enjoy yourself!

Allergies are, at best, unpleasant and uncomfortable. However, with sensible management and planning, it is possible to minimize the discomfort and live a happy, normal life.

Well-planned break

Good holiday planning is essential for people with allergies. Plan for the worst and then relax and enjoy the activities and adventure.

Glossary

adrenalin   a naturally occurring hormone that helps your body respond to stressful situations. It is used as a medicine to combat the effects of a severe allergic reaction.

allergen   a substance that causes an allergy.

allergy   a problem that occurs when your immune system reacts to a harmless substance as if it were a dangerous virus, bacterium or parasite.

anaphylaxis   a condition that can occur when you have a severe allergic reaction.

antibodies   protein molecules produced by the immune system that circulate around your body neutralizing bacteria and viruses.

antihistamine   a medicine used to treat the effects of a mild to moderate allergic reaction.

asthma   a disease that affects the airways in the lungs. The airways become inflamed and narrow and this makes breathing difficult. Asthma is usually caused by an allergy.

atopy   a genetic condition that means you are susceptible to developing allergies.

bacteria   minute single-cell organisms that can cause disease.

complementary therapy   a treatment used in addition to standard medical treatment, often to help the patient feel good about themselves or to reduce pain.

conjunctivitis   inflammation of the tissues surrounding the eye.

damp dusting   an efficient method of dusting, using a slightly dampened cloth. The moisture on the cloth traps the dust and prevents it from flying into the air.

dander   dead skin cells and feather scales that are shed by animals; the animal equivalent of human dandruff.

decongestant   a medicine that works to reduce the thickness of mucus produced in the nose and sinuses.

dermatitis   red and inflamed patches of skin caused by allergy or irritation.

desensitization   action taken to make your body less sensitive to a substance, so reducing the severity of an allergy.

diagnosis   the doctor's expert opinion about the name of the disease that is causing your problems.

eczema   a skin condition where the skin becomes hot and itchy, scales may form and the rash may weep a clear fluid.

emollients   softening and soothing substances to apply to the skin.

genes   parts of the genetic code present in each of your body cells, which controls the way your body grows and develops. You inherit your genetic code from your parents and pass it on to your children.

genetically inherited   passed from parents to children through genes. Characteristics such as eye and hair colour, and even whether we have a short temper, are passed on in this way.

hay fever   an allergic condition where pollen irritates the lining of the nose and causes sneezing and mucus production.

histamine   a chemical released in response to infection, allergy or injury, which results in inflammation.

hives   *see* urticaria.

homeopathy   a treatment that involves giving the person minute amounts of a substance which, in larger doses, would produce similar symptoms to those caused by their illness.

IgE   Immunoglobulin E, the antibody involved in allergies.

immune system   the body's defence system. It searches out and destroys viruses and bacteria, protecting you from infection.

inhaler   a gadget that allows medication to be inhaled directly to the lungs, where its effect is needed.

intradermal   into the top layers of the skin.

irritant   a substance that causes inflammation when it comes into contact with your body.

lymph node   a small organ in the lymph system, which is involved in the immune system.

lymphocyte   a type of white blood cell, which can produce antibodies.

mast cell   a cell that produces histamine when stimulated by an antibody.

mucus   fluid produced by the lungs and other mucous membranes in the body. When lungs are healthy, the mucus there is clear. If you have a chest infection, it may become thick or runny, green or yellow.

nebulizer   a piece of equipment that produces a mist of air. It is used to deliver medicine to the lungs.

non-steroidal anti-inflammatory drugs   medicines that reduce inflammation and do not contain steroids.

parasite   any organism that lives in or on another organism. In humans, these include tapeworms, thread worms, head lice, etc.

penicillin   an antibiotic medicine.

perennial rhinitis   constant inflammation in the nose, often caused by an allergy.

sinusitis   inflammation of the sinuses.

spores   the reproductive agents of moulds and fungi.

steroids   drugs that mimic the action of hormones, the body's natural steroids. They are often used to reduce inflammation and swelling.

urticaria   redness of the skin accompanied by small, flat, raised red spots.

virus   an infective agent that, once it gets inside a cell, reproduces and rapidly infects other cells. Viruses are responsible for many illnesses including the common cold, flu, chickenpox and herpes.

weal   a white or pinkish raised area of skin.

Resources

Organizations in the UK

British Allergy Foundation
Helpline 01322 619864

Registered charity aiming to improve awareness about the prevention and treatment of allergies.

Anaphylaxis Campaign
P O Box 275, Farnborough,
Hampshire GU14 6SX
Telephone 01252 542029

Provides information and support for people with anaphylaxis and their families, and lobbies for improvements to food labelling.

National Asthma Campaign
Providence House, Providence Place,
London N1 0NT
Telephone 0207 226 2260

This is an independent charity working with people with asthma to overcome the disease. It funds a great deal of research into asthma and offers education and support. Fact sheets, booklets, magazines and information packs for schools are available.

Asthma Help Line: 0845 701 0203
Run by the National Asthma Campaign, this help line is available Monday to Friday, 9am-7pm.

Medicalert
1 Bridge Wharf,
156 Caledonian Road,
London N1 9UU
Telephone 020 7833 3034

A charity which provides bracelets or necklaces engraved with essential medical information about the wearer, which a doctor would need to know before treating the person in an emergency.

Organizations in the USA

American Academy of Allergy Asthma and Immunology
555 East Wells Street, Suite 1100,
Milwaukee WI 53202-3823

American Lung Association
61 Broadway, 6th Floor,
NY, NY 10006

Provides useful information about all lung diseases and has many local centres around the USA.

Asthma and Allergy Foundation of America
1233 20th Street, NW, suite 402,
Washington DC 20036

Lots of research and information about all aspects of allergy and asthma.

The Food Allergy & Anaphylaxis Network
11781 Lee Jackson Hwy., Suite 160
Fairfax, VA 22033-3309

Provides information about living with food allergy and anaphylaxis.

Index

acupuncture 44

adrenalin injections 23, 40, 42, 43

aerosol sprays 28

air pollution 25

air quality 5

airways 9, 13, 14, 15, 25, 34, 35, 43

allergic illnesses 4, 5, 6, 7, 24, 25, 45 (*see also* asthma, conjunctivitis, hay fever, rhinitis, sinusitis, skin diseases)

allergies
  diagnosis 10-11
  how they start 8-9
  occupational 32, 56
  statistics 4, 13, 16, 17, 18, 21, 27, 31, 33
  treatments 10, 34-45

allergy clinics 13, 40, 41

anaphylaxis 4, 9, 10, 12, 17, 20, 22-3, 28, 29, 31, 33, 39, 40, 41, 42, 43, 50, 54
  treatment for 42-3

animal hair 14

antibiotics 35, 42

antibodies 7, 8, 9, 10, 12, 24 (*see also* IgE)

antihistamines 36, 37, 39, 44

antileukotrines 35

arachis oil 29, 49

asthma 4, 5, 6, 7, 9, 11, 13, 14-15, 21, 22, 27, 28, 29, 30, 31, 32, 44, 45, 47
  attacks 14-15, 34, 42, 44

rates, world 5, 15
  treatment 34-5, 42
  triggers 14, 15

atopy 6

bee stings 8, 9 (*see also* insect stings)

blood pressure 9, 43

blood tests 12

B-lymphocytes 8, 9

breast-feeding 24

bronchoprovocation 13

cats 11

challenge tests 12-13

chemicals 7, 28, 32, 51, 57

cleaning products 28, 51-2

cleanliness 5, 13

cockroaches 27, 50-1

colds 24, 25

complementary therapies 44-5

conjunctivitis 20, 37

cosmetics 29, 55

cough(ing) 9, 15, 19, 24, 25, 32, 36

cross reactivity 27, 33

dairy products 21, 48

dander 6, 11, 20, 27, 50

decongestants 36

dermatitis, contact 17, 32, 38-9

desensitization 37, 40, 41

detergents 5, 28, 58

diarrhoea 9, 20, 22

dust mites 5, 9, 14, 16, 18, 20, 26, 33, 46-7, 52

ears 19

eczema 6, 7, 9, 11, 25, 29, 38-9, 58
  atopic 16-17
  'wet' 17

eggs 17, 21, 22, 29, 33, 48

emollients 38

environment 6, 7, 13, 24, 25, 26

exercise 44

eyes 9, 18, 20, 28, 32, 37, 51, 55

feathers 20, 27, 33, 57

fish 21, 29, 49

flu 24

food allergies 4, 6, 11, 13, 20-1, 29, 40, 48-50, 59

food intolerance 21-2

foods 16, 20, 22, 29, 33, 40, 48-50, 51, 58

gas, cooking 29, 53

genes 6, 7, 24

genetic makeup 4

glues 28

hay fever 4, 6, 7, 9, 11, 13, 18, 30, 36, 41, 57 (*see also* rhinitis)

heart 9

herbal medicines 45

histamines 8, 9, 35, 36

ALLERGIES

hives 9, 17, 29, 32, 39
holidays 58-9
homeopathy 45
hypoallergenic 52

IgE (Immunoglobulin E) 7, 8, 9, 12
illness 25 (*see also* allergic illnesses)
immune system 6, 7, 8, 9, 13, 15, 21, 22, 24, 25, 29, 31, 35, 36, 41
industrialized nations 5
inhalers 11, 34, 35
insect stings 6, 22, 31, 54, 59
irritants 28, 51

kerosene 29, 53

latex 17, 22, 32, 33, 53, 56, 59
lungs 13, 14, 15, 19, 28, 35

mast cells 8, 9, 35
mast cell stabilizers 35, 36, 37
Medicalert 43, 53
medicines (as allergens) 17, 22, 28, 35

milk 21, 22, 24, 29, 48
moulds 5, 9, 14, 18, 20, 30, 52, 54

nasal challenge test 13
nickel 17
nose 9, 18, 19, 28, 51, 55
nut allergies 6, 20, 22, 29, 49

oral challenge test 13

paints 28
peanuts 6, 21, 22, 23, 24, 29, 49
perfume 17, 51, 55, 58
pet hair 9, 16, 18, 20, 27, 50, 58
pets 6, 27, 50, 56
pollen 4, 6, 8, 9, 14, 16, 18, 19, 20, 30-1, 45, 55-6, 58
pollution 7 (*see also* air pollution)

rash 7, 9, 16, 17, 22, 26, 35, 39, 42, 51, 58 (*see also* hives, urticaria)
rhinitis, allergic 4, 9, 13, 18, 19, 20, 21, 29, 30, 36, 37, 44, 47 (*see also* hay fever)

royal jelly 45

shellfish 21, 22, 29
shrimps 33
sinuses 19, 20, 37
sinusitis 4, 19-20, 37
skin 5, 8, 10, 11, 16, 17, 26, 28, 38, 46, 54
skin diseases, allergic 16-17
skin tests 10-11, 12, 41, 46
smoking 25
sneezing 9, 18, 19, 24, 25, 32
soya 21, 29, 50
spina bifida 33
steroid medication 35, 36, 37, 38, 39, 42
strawberries 4, 7, 17
stress 24, 25

throat 19, 20, 42

urticaria 17, 20, 39

viruses 24, 25
virus infections 24-5
vomiting 9, 20

wheat 21, 29, 50
workplace 32, 33, 56-7